Bob the Builder™

Who Can Fix It?

Activity Book

CBeebies BBC

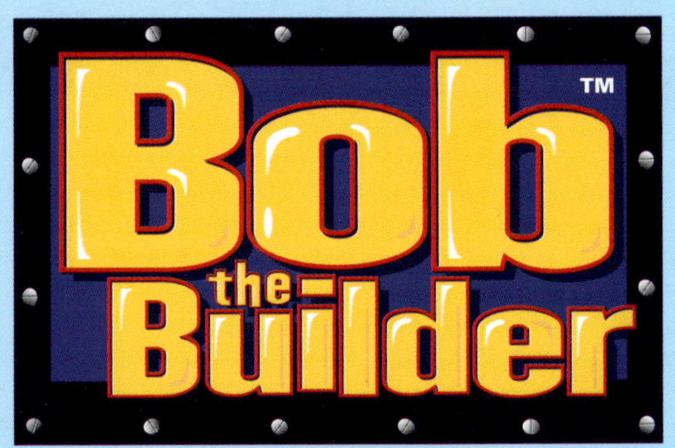

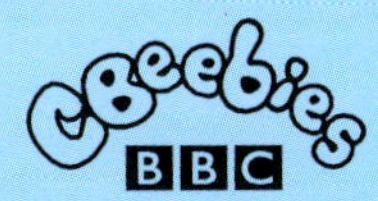

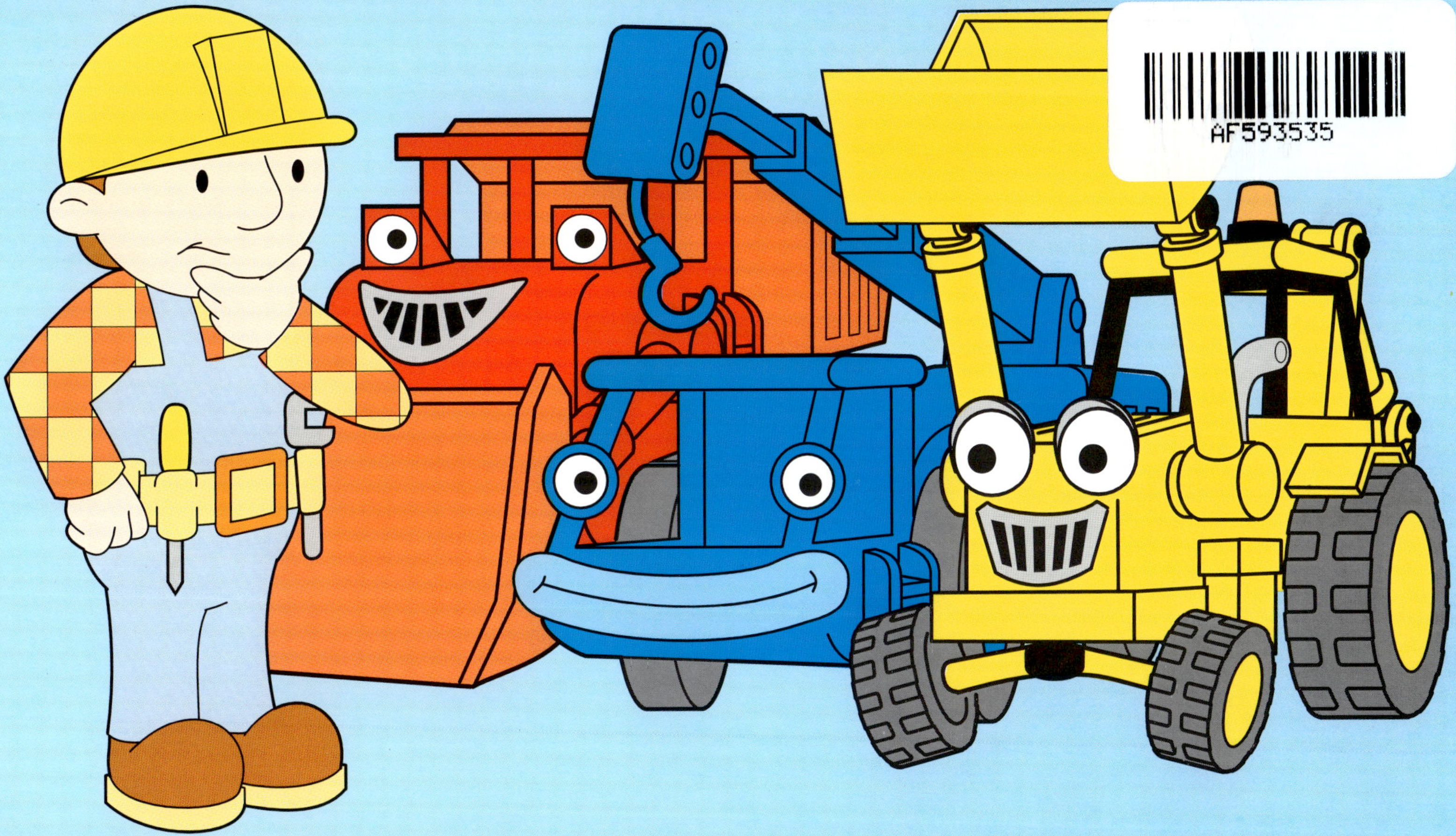

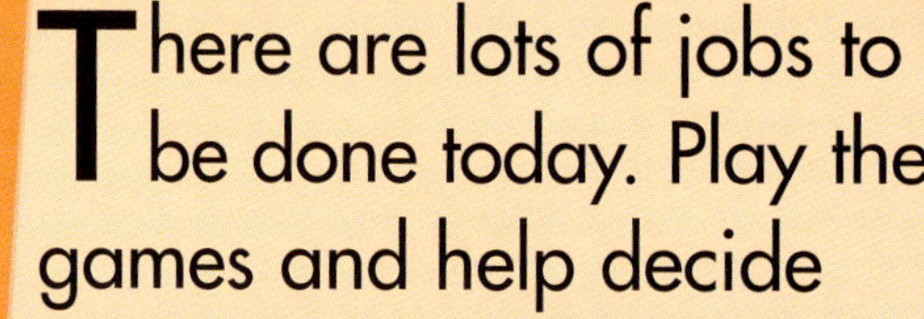

There are lots of jobs to be done today. Play the games and help decide

WHO CAN FIX IT?

The drainpipe at the farmhouse has cracked. Wendy needs a machine to help her lift these new pipes into place.

Draw a circle around the machine you think would be best for the job.

WHO CAN LIFT IT?

LOFTY CAN
LIFT IT!
Did you get it right?
Colour in the scene.

There are six small visitors hiding in Bob's yard. Can you find them?
WHO CAN CHASE THEM?

PILCHARD CAN CHASE THEM!
Pilchard loves chasing mice. Can you draw some for her to scare away? Colour in Pilchard's face and stripes using the little picture to help you.

Farmer Pickles needs to take some vegetables to the market. Who should he take with him?

These parts belong to the machine that can help.

Can you find the shadow of the right machine?

WHO CAN CARRY IT?

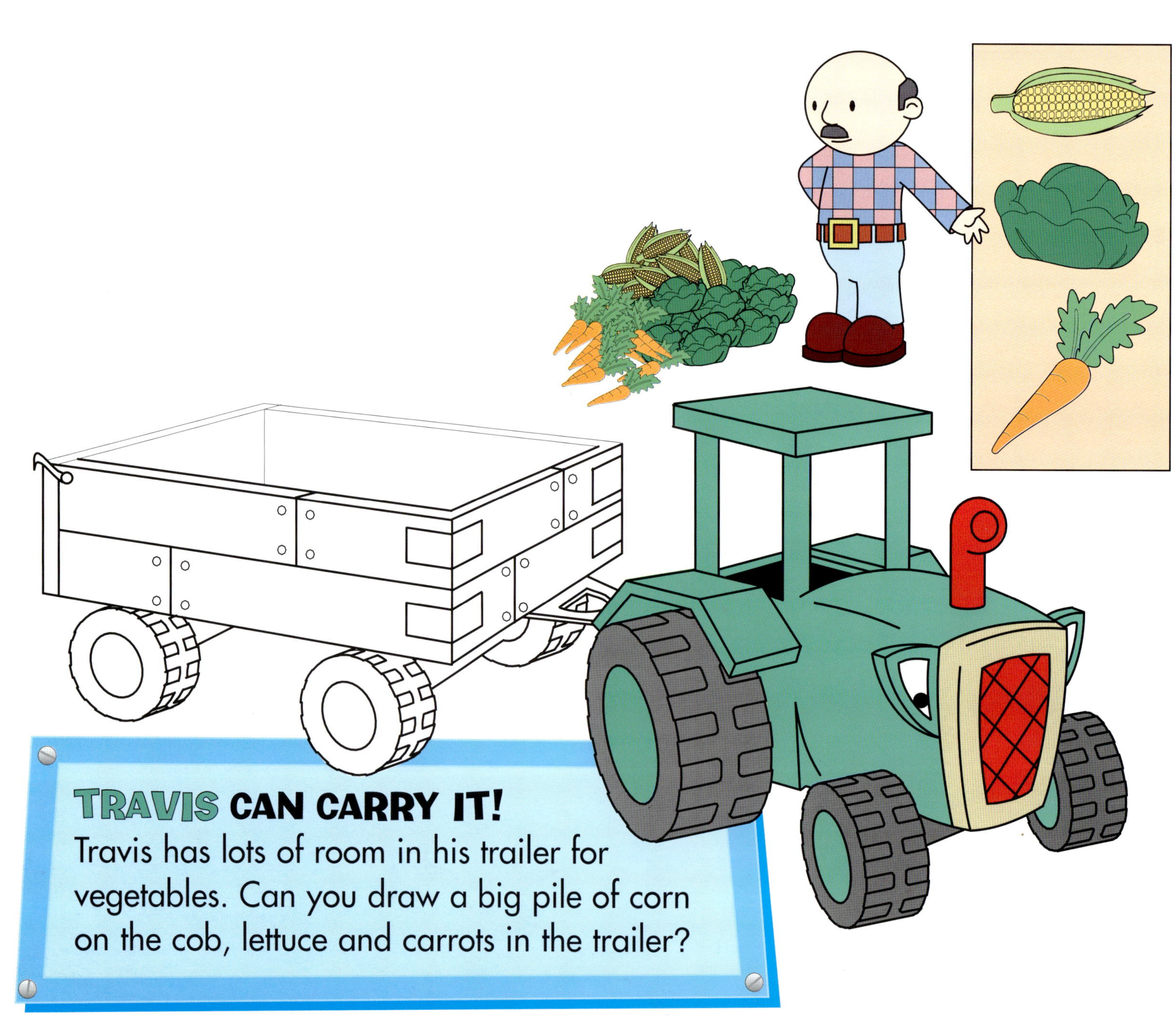

TRAVIS CAN CARRY IT!

Travis has lots of room in his trailer for vegetables. Can you draw a big pile of corn on the cob, lettuce and carrots in the trailer?

There are lots of jobs to do around the yard.
The window frames need painting.
The fence needs mending.
The door hinge needs fixing.
The yard needs sweeping.

WHO CAN FIX IT?

BOB CAN FIX IT!

Which tool should he use for each task? Draw a line to join the job on the top to the right tool on the bottom.

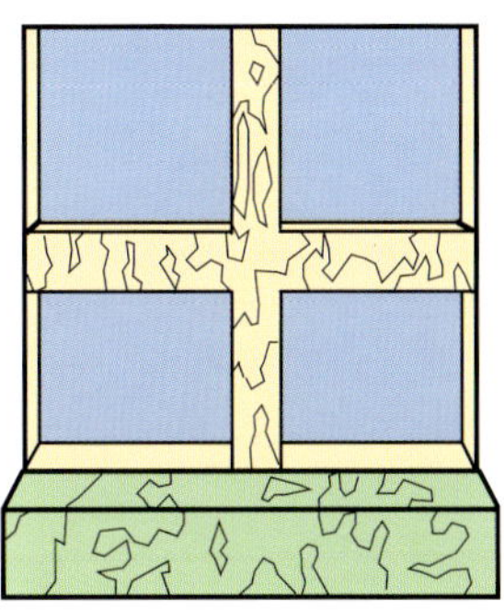

Bob is in the office. He wants to print some letters, but he's in a muddle.

WHO CAN HELP HIM?

Who should he call to help him use the computer? Look at the phone list. Can you find the right numbers to press on the phone?

Mrs Potts
5437

Farmer Pickles
7612

Wendy's mobile
6893

WENDY CAN HELP HIM!

She knows all about computers.
Can you colour her in?

The road outside the town hall needs to be resurfaced. Find the street that needs fixing and follow the line to find out who can make it nice and flat.

WHO CAN ROLL IT?

ROLEY CAN ROLL IT!

Did you get it right? Join the dots to finish the picture.

Birds are eating Farmer Pickles's seeds. How many birds can you count? He needs some help to scare them away. There's someone hiding in the picture who can help.
WHO CAN SCARE THEM?

SPUD CAN SCARE THEM!

Did you get it right? Can you draw in Spud's missing half?

Bob is building a swimming pool. He needs help moving the mud that Scoop has dug. Who should Bob ask? The machine that can help has these parts.

WHO CAN SHIFT IT?

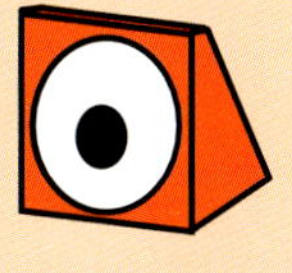

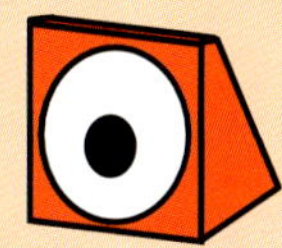

2 eyes

2 caterpillar treads

1 front digger

1 back dumper

MUCK CAN SHIFT IT!

Muck is great at shovelling mud.

There are six differences between these two pictures. Can you spot what they are?

A trench needs digging for some new pipes to be laid. The right machine for the job is the same colour as the things below.

WHO CAN DIG IT?

Wendy's hair

Hay bale

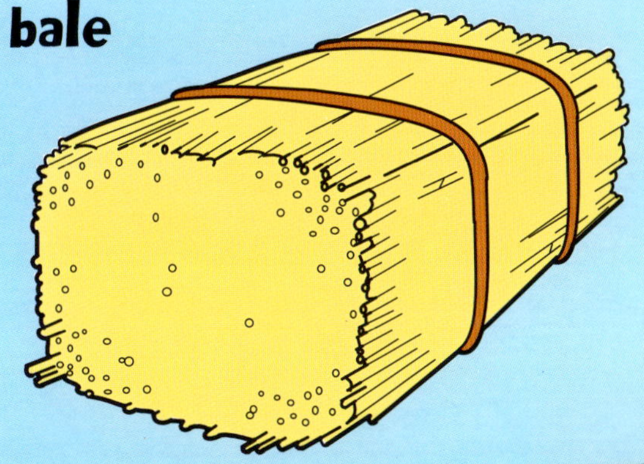

Skip

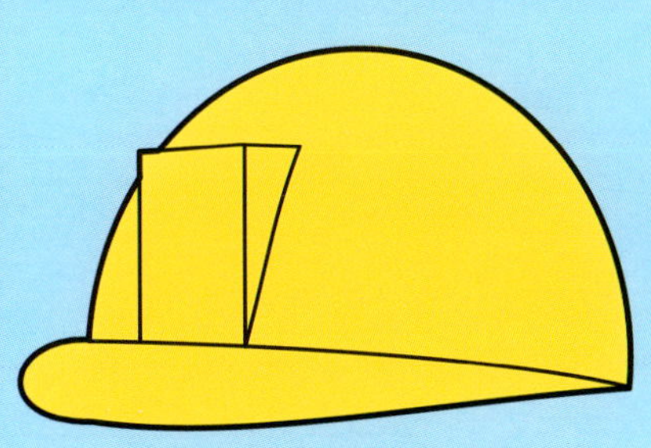

Bob's hat

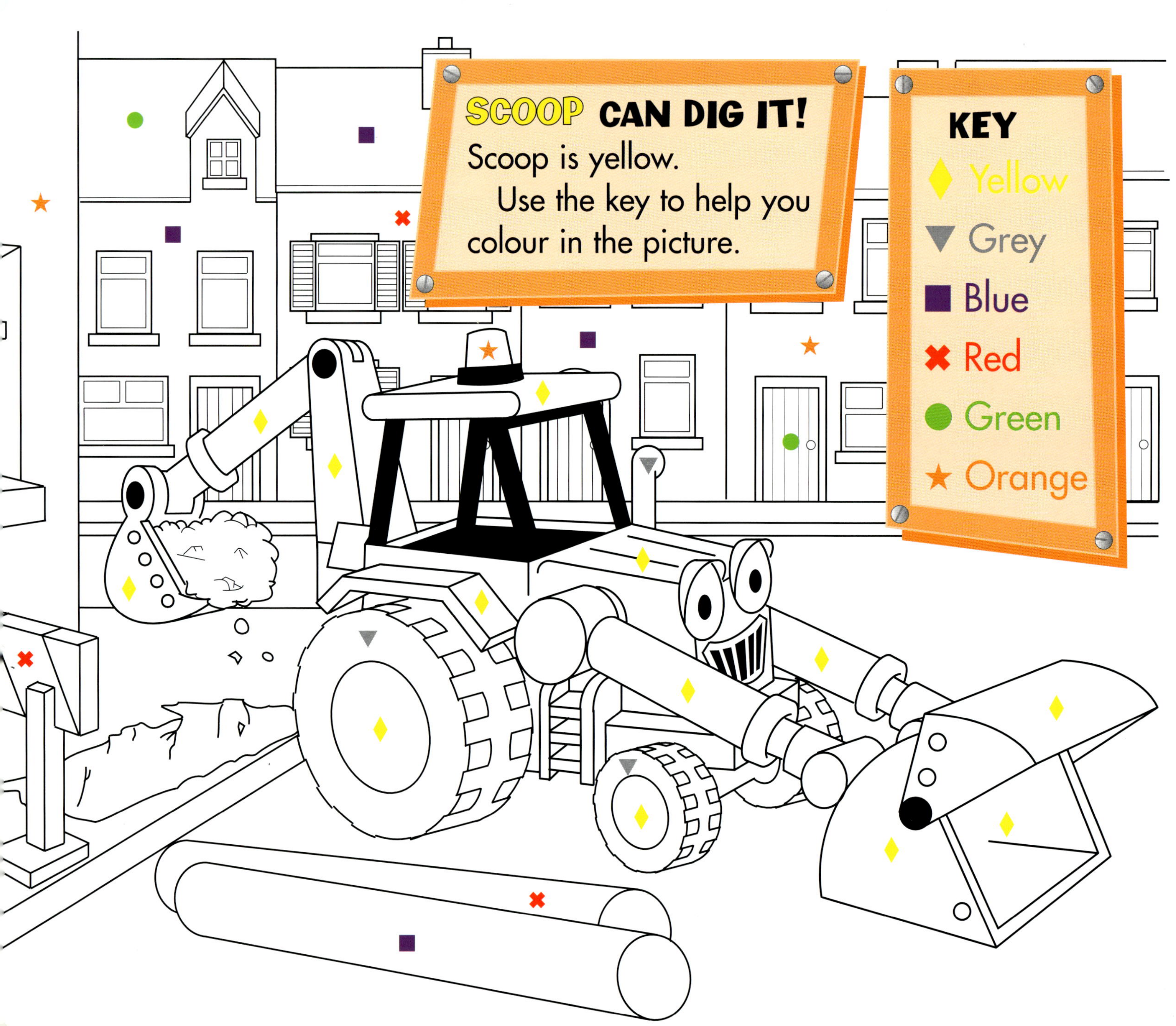
SCOOP CAN DIG IT!
Scoop is yellow.
Use the key to help you colour in the picture.
KEY
Yellow
Grey
Blue
Red
Green
Orange

Bob is building a patio. He needs some cement to lay the slabs. Which machine should he choose to mix the water, sand and gravel?
WHO CAN MIX IT?

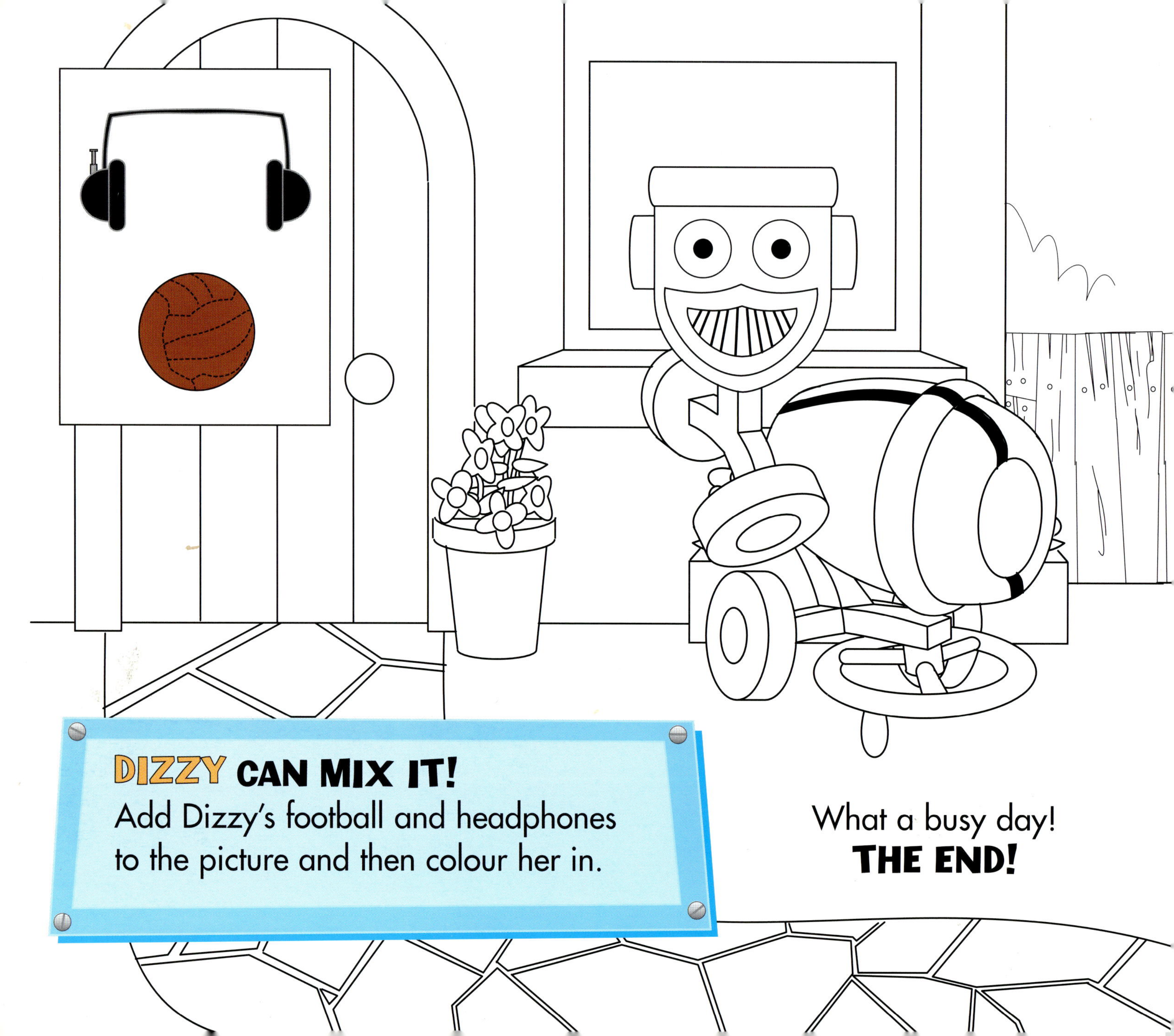

DIZZY CAN MIX IT!

Add Dizzy's football and headphones to the picture and then colour her in.

What a busy day!

THE END!